DATE DUE

Demco, Inc. 38-293

ENTERED APR 7 2009

WHS

Realm Sixty-four

ahsahta press

The New Series

number 21

Realm Sixty-four

Kristi Maxwell

AHSAHTA PRESS

Boise State University • Boise • Idaho • 2008

Ahsahta Press, Boise State University
Boise, Idaho 83725
http://ahsahtapress.boisestate.edu

Library of Congress Cataloging-in-Publication Data

Maxwell, Kristi.
Realm sixty-four / Kristi Maxwell.
    p. cm. -- (The new series ; no. 21)
ISBN 978-0-916272-97-5 (pbk. : alk. paper)
I. Title.
PS3613.A916R43 2008
811'.6—dc22

                    2007012572

ACKNOWLEDGMENTS

Grateful acknowledgment is made to the editors of the following journals in which these poems, sometimes in earlier versions, first appeared: *580 Split* (thank you, Loretta Clodfelter), *Dragonfire* (thank you, Henry Israeli), *How2* (thank you, Kate Fagan), *Tarpaulin Sky* (thank you, Christian Peet), *Typo* (thank you, Adam Clay and Matthew Henriksen), and *Phoebe* (thank you, Shawn Flanagan).

Special thanks to Dan Beachy-Quick, who chose "the first chess-playing automaton: the Turk" as winner of the 2005 Margaret Sterling Award in Poetry, and to the University of Arizona Poetry Center, which produced a limited edition broadside of the poem.

To all those who coaxed, cared for, and challenged—thank you, with special thanks to Jane Miller, Tenney Nathanson, Boyer Rickel, Ashley VanDoorn, Marty Hebrank, Sommer Browning, Melissa Koosmann, Tony Mancus, Theresa Sotto, Ann Fine, and Kristen Nelson. For first pushes, thanks to Arthur Smith, Marilyn Kallet, and Richard Jackson. Thank you also to Janet Holmes and everyone at Ahsahta.

I also wish to thank my family, Marilyn, Ken, Jennifer, and Lori, and the sweetest etcetera who have expanded my notion of family.

for Michael Rerick

Contents

Mate

A heart hawked into a napkin / whose heart—?

Body wadded up

the only position in which you slept.

So queen- and king-pieces do look like blossomed pawns

and pawns send me reminiscing of your knees

held near your body like folded clothes—

have you moved yet?

My anesthesia's no good without your blade.

Let's say I won't win

that I bury landmines in time so each day is a challenge to run through.

That's not right either. I say time as in "had a good / bad"

a fence around the past tense / No Trespassing.

Constellations are so predictable—you think we'd be tired

of night / the way stars hold their light as if it were precious—

tongue-toughened thumbs of light.

We had talked about it once. Someone said will?

Someone said yes. Someone said

fate is a conscious will—a barge that leads a cruise ship out of harbor.

My yes barged in on.

I've lowered a cutout of you into my mine (you're standing

in a field where we before or after made love / for the sake of saying so

where what would have been a sheep

but were only sheep bones

laid close enough to your head they might have been / bedposts).

The lights are blinking on and off—

is it alright to move closer / if someone's left? Despite

assigned seats? (fate's

not gonna like it) Usher, usher us.

the first chess-playing automaton: the Turk

built by Wolfgang von Kempelen

Part One: von Kempelen's background

       (task: translate Hungarian civil code from Latin to German, 1755)

To sit language inside ink and let it punch out letters
like a fetal hand, or foot—feel it kicking
the mouth into sound.

       (task: decipher the nature of Pelletier's conjuring tricks, 1769)

Easy.

As if dry-ice ghosts water

but the room's cold, not companied.

What difference to skin—

it rises like cake,

o delicious belief!—scrutiny scrapes out

my tongue—

Part Two:

(task: carry out the claim, *I can build a machine—its deception much
more complete*)

Six months, then debut, 1770—*my wooden man
before his wooden men—no, not you—(not even the queen's
so impeccably chiseled)—no, no name—he will name himself,*

name-hemmed, the clothes pinned around him, the cape,
and a thin pipe lengthened through his fingers like a carving
of a wave, its crest red carpet rolled, or rolling.

　　　—so
a small casket, un-drawered from a drawer in the box
behind which the wooden man sits.

From time to time, peeked into,
as if a spectacle hatchery,
as if von Kempelen expects

crack—every cabinet's opened, faces look through
to other faces, each face looks
into the mechanical chest, lunged with cogs—

inspection faced with satisfaction,
the Turk nods his opponent
the first move, man before invention—

knob and door, then knob-ignorant door:
motion sensed, a door slides open
minus the hand.

Part Three: The invention invincible, the Turk tours

(tour #1: Knight's, in which each square is visited once, and only once)

This is where the board is most field-like,
the Knight more shape-like than name-.
A horse, and a handful of peas.

Gallop, land—pea.
Gallop, land—pea, or sometimes a red counter,
a small coin—hoof marks.

Spectator fence, loose around the board.
The back hoof knocks a little
at a high jump, near the end—

where's the square, untouched,
how can my body L me there—
lunge, leap, lash, lessen me
that I might alight.

(tour #2: Europe, *urged* by the emperor)

Damn the Turk—it's my time's corset, the emperor
in the back, tugging
and tying—

                but it must be me,
or its secret gnawed through like foiled chocolate—
good chocolate at that—dropped outside the door—

those Rats! Illusion a taste that can't be trusted
without its ingredients deciphered—
must *to know* cancel out *to believe*?

the Turk *v* Napoleon (true, 2-1)

the Turk *v* Catherine the Great (untrue, though she lost, twice)

   v Johann von Goethe (true)

   v Beethoven, Ben Franklin (true, true)

   v truth (truth *v* true, *i.e.* it is the truth that curtains are the room's jaws

        that chomp, or widen, but not true the sky fears swallow

        anymore than a pillow is a muscle flexed by sleep—

        this understood, when the Turk *v* truth, applause

        is the opponents shaking hands)

Scientific *v* Illusory (game in progress)

Wonder *v* Proof (though nine hundred and seven known articles were printed

disputing the Turk's mechanism, crowds continued to be satisfied

by a spin of the box as one delights over a dessert tray

though each sample's shaped with shortening—

belief monocles and magnifies perspective,

so that even a fly's wing might be

the brooch air wears—want

bubble-wraps every

perhaps)

* * *

Part Four: All this is marvelous, but—a self-moving machine?

(theory)

hidden under the chessb(magnet)oar(magnet)d—the opponent's moves dip the oar below the surface where a dwarf or child or a legless man waits to intercept it—a pet anticipating crumbs—it is one of their hands, the current that steers the next move

(theory)

hidden in von Kempelen's left-hand coat(magnet)pock(magnet)et—he moves, and his invention's arm raises, a chess-piece in its fingers—and the board?—artifice is a rash someone misdiagnoses game

(theory)

controlled by strings—as if light-rays anchor the sun—or a road is a leash direction yanks—or your lips a knot sound wriggles out of—or the drain is a water lasso—or the ground a grass harness—or your line of vision, the horizon sucks like a straw

(theory)

chest hollowed,
a human concealed—
thought skeleton,
bone-skilled

Part Five: Johann Nepomuk Maelzel rebuilds and improves the Turk, operated
primarily by his attendant Schlumberger

Triangle—you become, paper folded, then cut,
a snowflake. Only your globe isn't glass. Isn't even a globe,
but a wooden box.

Its drawer built short, to hold you,
to hide you behind. A chessboard-painted tray folds out—

zombie's arms. The un-living made live
by your movement.

Do you remember when they yelled fire—fire! and all
you could do was cinch
your breath like a garbage bag.
If weight tears through. Call it back, call back your body—

how did he bring you to? That you trusted him to save you.
His fame was a flame you wouldn't pinch.
Love a machine cranked to flank your sneeze—
your pupil tightened like a gear,

yes, it's the light. The beeswax candle
on your right—when your opponent longed over his move,
letters waxed on your woolen thigh—

surely, you knew he'd notice peeled flakes at your seat
as he helped you out. How many candles before he found his name?

* * *

Fire—you did not heave your body like a chair
through the flap, but waited, heart clicking
like the knob the two of you used to communicate,
a numbered knob as on a safe. Practical numbers,
sure: nine, *wax-drowned wick*; three, *please re-set*
the last move on the middle of its square. Please.
What private numbers? five, *hold me like this box*;
two, *my knees peak, and I wonder, does the sun ache*
when it's night-punctured by orbit; tonight let's practice
erosion, it's my turn as weather.

Part Six: Maelzel's defense, verbatim & otherwise

What I said on our ride was I like what happens—
What Happens is you—

not hoax, but illusion,

for example, not untrue: *I live my life*—can I be blamed *I* and *my*
aren't differentiated,
which operator, and which machine—

can I
be blamed

to live is considered action, rather than result?

* * *

Pittsburgh-bound, Maelzel booked a private cabin.

As a bird flies south, so does Fortune—the sun gold-traces
what blocks it—his outline on the ship-deck
from Havana.

Pawns tucked like a rosary into his pocket, he chose his throat
a mausoleum for a marble-born king.

What is yellow? Butter. Gold, in certain paintings, or at least
what the shimmer shatters into is yellow, a tint of it.
Schlumberger yellowed with fever.

Fortune missed like a decimal placed one space
too far to the right—

less in its more-masquerade, and someone shortchanged.
When S. died, Maelzel boarded a ship—

Correspondence Game

between Maelzel & Schlumberger

20 December 1825[1]

S—

You asked what I hear when my Panharmonicon[2] plays—

I can only imagine
you want an answer other than sound.

What if I said I feel your hair? I'm afraid you'd be disappointed—
to want the mind, but receive only its cap.

It is not your hair.

I would describe the notes to you as hands screeching from a painting's inferno—
before you distort my observation—the music is hell—know
the painting's displayed in a cathedral, so if the notes hang in your ears,

this is how I praise your body.

Do you suppose an egg prefers a nest to a plate? I enclose my move—
N-KB3—that it might beak open my victory, and flap around. Crack suggests
your hand—should you hope to guide the break—

were this not

---

[1] The previous day, before M. boarded the packet ship *Howard* for New York, M. and S. made their
first moves in a chess game they agreed to finish through correspondence during their separation. M.,
who chose the white pawn from S.'s right hand from behind his back, moved first: P-K4. S. followed
with P-K4. This letter was delivered, for the fee of an orange, by a dockhand soon after departure.

[2] A musical automaton, consisting of mechanical players, ranging from trumpeter to cellist, though
these musicians were in the shape of copper pegs that rotated on a cylinder, as found in a music box.
To call his invention a music box would be misleading—much more a music crate, measuring 6 x 6
x 5 feet.

a game, I would be a passive yolk—your action
could supersede my own.

Yours—

28 December 1825

Sir—

I keep telling the hours to stop slouching,
so there's no sway in the time between us—

I'm pausing my skin.

You were wrong, that I would be disappointed.

Christmas was a carriage ride—I read the paper—letters strung
across the page, the only tree that caught me—my hand, clutching it,
any other ornament—your hand would have been a star, gold-foiled.

A woman[3] unthreaded a grass-blade
and put it in her husband's drink—his throat sliced
like a paper lantern.

Do you suppose flint feels sorry
or envy for a match?

Perhaps both—I move my knight to the queen's bishop's
third rank—I suspected the Lopez Opening.

Faithfully—

---

[3] The verdict for Natasha Gronsky, accused of sabotaging her husband's tea, was decided on 23 December 1825 and printed in papers across Europe, one of which it is assumed S. purchased before his return to Vienna. She was found, to the surprise of most, not guilty, due to the traveling nature of grass, which often finds its way, thanks to wind, into one's kitchen, particularly if a window is left opened, as neighbors testified the Gronskys' often was.

14 April 1826[4]

S—

I scanned the audience for your face as one does his memory
for a name—

but you are more my tongue than what tips it—

I swore, & the swearing's a hot coal
I can no longer hold in my mouth—come!

It's pretzels here, on the street, twisted, tucked, so there's no end—
this isn't what Aristophanes meant.

The sun spilt its light today, and it took until night to gather—
listen—I remember what you told me about the trapdoor[5] spider

that fangs the door closed

until the right feet trill across. I'm holding my ear out like a flower,
be the bee that ransacks the rose.

Yours, & I move my queen's pawn to the fourth rank—

---

[4] On April 13, the Turk played its first game in New York City. Between the time of this letter and the prior in this collection, there was a telegram from M. to S. that read "Lopez. Yes. B-N5," after which, S., distressed at the coldness America had produced in his partner, replied with a letter that contained neither a salutation nor a signature, but a move—P-Q3. Due to the recognition of his offense, the next two letters exchanged contained apologies, etc., but no moves; thus their absence.

[5] Many speculated, incorrectly, that an operator entered the Turk after the audience scrutinized its wide-flung cabinet doors through a covered opening in the floor. Several pet-names developed after S. and M. mocked the incorrect theories of the Turk's secrets, including "my trap," stemming, of course, from trapdoor, to which the letter's mention might allude, along with "mag," which is an abbreviated form of either "magic" or, and often considered more plausible because of the hard "g," "magnet."

5 May 1826

My sir—

That I've hung a sign in the store's window.[6]

Last night, I dreamt of your eye—and the lashes that rim it
were stones—a burial ground
desecrated with movement—someone said *ghost*,
then, more loudly, *Ghost*—

and we laughed as I danced even more wildly
in that blue circle
until veins rose to the occasion

and flooded my skin.

You put your hand there, and I thought you might   .[7]

I board the *Pensero* tomorrow,
I plank our board now: our first capture, my pawn claims
your queen's pawn.

Faithfully—

---

[6] Translation: *I agree to come.* Because S. did not own a store, or even work at a store for that matter, one must conclude this line is metaphoric. If the "store's window" is his face, then the sign might be a smile, or, more literally, because sea voyages were known to dry one's face to the point of discomfort, the sign could be read as a salve, whose use was recommended up to five days before a voyage.

[7] Time has not preserved the word that graced this space. Though, given the context, some propose: *float, drown, drain, lily-pad* (used as an unorthodox verb), or *raft*. One reading interprets the missing word(s) as *part me*, an allusion to the biblical Red Sea, but neither of the men was given to religious whims, so this reading is criticized, though it does bounce nicely off the translation of the first line, as, in order "to come" or "to go," one must first *part* his present company.

8 May 1826[8]

My.

Yes, my.

I have turned my pocket watch into a locket—
you are all the time.

The locket startles into a mouth—we talk,

my tongue a chandelier
hung on the first syllable of your name.

What is the locket but a heart imitation? Down the street, a company
announces "An Imitation of Mister Maelzel's Chess-Player"—

two shillings less. My fickle audience, I can't blame them—
don't I spotlight a picture of your face

as if it were your face—

I fill my bleachers.

Where is the ax—that I've been gazing across the ocean
when I need only puncture my stomach

---

[8] This letter was sent before the 5 May 1826 letter arrived and does not contain a move for that reason.
It is included in this collection because it illustrates the mental fragility that demanded S.'s presence,
though S. decided to join M. before this state was made apparent to him, suggesting a devotion
beyond necessity, but also a psychic connection, as S. had originally planned to leave on a ship at the
beginning of June, but pushed his departure up, despite a downgrade in cabin and an invitation to a
court birthday, where there would have undoubtedly been cake.

and you rapunzel out in the guise of an intestine,

yes—my.

[12 June 1826]

Gums[9] , how can you lose me—you've witnessed the miracle of teeth.

—B-Q2[10]

---

[9] When his ship arrived in New York, S., with an uncanny amount of coyness, perhaps suffering a bit from cabin fever, had this note run by a dock-boy to M.'s address. This is the only note in this collection in which S. unguards his formal "sir" that had, by this time, become its own term of endearment.

[10] This move suggests S. intuited M. would follow S.'s P x QP with N-Q4 x P, which we know to be true based on M.'s game notation, which marks this move as made on 8 June 1826, four days before S.'s arrival.

20 June 1826

S—

If you go a block east on Milk Street[11] from the intersection
of Congress & Milk,

there's a clairvoyant whom I gave my hands.

She tugged me to the roof, and pointed—
the lines in my palms were town center

and I felt my future peddling
on a corner—

no, it was holding someone's wares to light
and discovering rust-gnawed holes.

Have you looked at the lines in your hands—
dismantled stickmen—

who would it take to command them,
stand up & walk—that they'd roll up your body

a cot under their arms.

I will be home by Sunday; until then my knight
captures your queen's knight,

Thoughtfully—

---

[11] Written on M.'s Boston trip, during which he booked Julien Hall, located on Milk Street, where the
Turk would begin performances in September. S. carried out some private performances during M.'s
absence, as per request. The operator during these shows is unknown.

[Tuesday, Au]gust [1826][12]

Plank to replace cracked Plank on moving crate

Peacock feather[13]

Tea[14]

send latest Articles and Flyers to [my and Maelzel's] families

Rubber Tubing, Sheet Music and Black Ink, Whatever Paint looks closest to Flame

---

[12] This date is based on the time of the week errands were traditionally run, along with the fragment "gust," which also suggests wind's presence and action—an almanac shows August most embodies those months affected. Because M. and S. were so infrequently apart after S. joined him in the Americas, they had no need to send letters to one another. The anticipation to complete the game, however, was not quelled by their proximity; thus alternate ways, such as lists, were developed to pass on one's next move.

[13] This refers not only to the decoration in the Turk's turban that likely needed a replacement, but also to S.'s acknowledgment that though M. was the showy one, it was S. himself that birthed the Turk into awe—M. the decoration, and S. the bone structure.

[14] Though tea for drinking would have been one of its uses, it also hints at M.'s self-training at reading tealeaves after his experience with the Boston fortune-teller. Apparently, his readings were quite knowledgeable, which can be seen in the following example: after he identified a dog in S.'s leaves, S. recalled where in his brain an address was buried and retrieved it, profiting himself and M. by obtaining an invitation for the Turk, wherein the Turk challenged the last living signer of the Declaration of Independence, Charles Carroll, who made the famous quip: *If the mind can declare independence from the body, then the Turk is the paper on which it is writ.*

accept Farewell demonstration with Greco[15]

capture M's Knight with my Own[16]

Need more Soap, but a Small Size, or Travel with It?

---

[15] Before their sweep from New York City to Boston, a leading New York chess-player, Greco—one of the few let in on the Turk's secret, after his adamant and intrusive claims of Americans' skills in comparison to Europeans', which it should be noted were quieted after M. suggested Greco settle for a game with S. rather than the Turk, at which S. beat him in under twenty moves—arranged a demonstration to raise money for his chess club. To suggest blackmail is either far off, or very close.

[16] One can assume the list would be returned to M. at the day's end, at which time he would slash a mental line through each completed task, leaving only S.'s move, which M. would carry out in the presence of S. We know, based on the game's final notation that M. already had his counter-move prepared, and excitement would not let him wait for ink—because both moves are marked on each opponent's sheet with the same pressure of quill-tip, along with equal slant of letters and symbols, it's guessed he moved his piece to B-QR4 within a minute. To which S., as quickly, to up the intuition-ante, moved N-KB3.

20 October 1828[17]

S—

Again, the sea—America and Europe
paddles I'm knocked between.

Where's the net—that I must make it over?
Rivalry net, Net-Which-Amazes,
Net-My-Imagination's-Poached-In.

Have you ever considered porpoises as rifles
waves sling?

Reconsider[18] —isn't the shot anticipated if the weapon's known?
The artillery our competition manufactures in its brain factory.

If I could I'd finger the hieroglyphs
that must wall my thinking, and decipher a message
from the pictures:

doesn't that look like your hand, and what's
it holding? A bronze-bent bird that cranks an incubated egg
into its wire nest—

---

[17] This is not the next move that transpired in the correspondence game, but the previous list is considered a representative for all moves that occurred between the aforementioned document and this one. Those moves that occurred followed an approximate month-long intermission between them: see index for moves eight through twelve. This letter was written on a ship to Europe to S., who stayed behind on a tour circuit of Boston, Philadelphia, and New York.

[18] Though this seems an answer to his question, along with an admonition to change that answer, it is more likely a plea to change S.'s mind about returning to his homeland of France, where he hoped to secure a job that would allow him to provide some financial alleviation for M.

my imagination's a clipped wing,
be my cage if for nothing than to wreck my flight.

Not me, but what I'm kept in.

Yours, & I castle, king's-side—

20 December 1828

M—

Snow fattens the roads—or else it's scar tissue
warmth exfoliates.[19]

I hope invention is the catgut with which you're sutured and home[20]
the ointment.

At last evening's show, an exploitationist asked
for his opaque fabric patched
against the Turk's chest

to assert his claim
an operator observed the board
from there—

we mocked him, lightly, and asserted too the viability
the heart uses skin as a magnifying glass—
that something burns through—*is* burned through.

These are little victories.

---

[19] Because either option would be considered positive coming from S., as he needed to gain at least five pounds after a month-long sickness that preceded the season change, and, for scar tissue to be exfoliated, it suggests a disappearance, most likely due to healing, it is accepted that this is how S. answered M.'s plea to reconsider—an affirmative answer.

[20] A literal interpretation: Europe. An abstract interpretation: M.'s own person. A generic interpretation: the place in which one's growth occurred. A literal interpretation of growth: noted by age- and inch-count. A non-literal interpretation: noted by the head from which one's life philosophy springs.

As for your "bronze-bent bird," would the egg
hatch-persist?

I confess, I hoped it inedible—
that the imaginary parents the real.

Patiently, as my knight takes your king's pawn[21]—

---

[21] This is the last move recorded in addition to its accompanying correspondence, though, because the game's complete notation (see index) was found in M.'s documents, we know the game was completed in 1833, three years before their deaths.

Index: the Correspondence Game's Final Notation

1.	P-K4	P-K4
2.	N-KB3	N-QB3
3.	B-N5	P-Q3
4.	P-Q4	P x QP
5.	N-Q4 x P	B-Q2
6.	N x QN	KNP x N
7.	B-QR4	N-KB3
8.	N-QB3	QB-KN5
9.	P-KB3	QB-KR4
10.	KB-QB6 CH.	N-Q2
11.	KB x QR	Q x KB
12.	N-Q5	N-KB3
13.	O-O	N x KP
14.	N x QBP CH.	K-Q1
15.	N x Q	P-Q4
16.	Q-Q5 CH.	K-Q1
17.	Q x QB	KB-QB4 CH.
18.	QB-K3	P-KN3
19.	Q-KN4	N-Q7
20.	KR-Q1	B-K6 CH.
21.	K-KR	KR-K1
22.	Q-QB7 mate	

Evergreen Game

When we play chess, we partake of the eternal,
because chess concepts depend on formal relations.
—Fred Reinfeld, *The Human Side of Chess*

1. e4

played in 1852, only later called
"the evergreen in Adolph Anderssen's laurel wreath"
though he had no wreath—the Father of
World Championship Chess
played the game in 2-3 hours at a café,

e5

pieces jutting toward the ceiling
like little toes: which gets privileged with wiggle?

went   *went*   *went*

it was a treat when father popped my toes

2. Nf3

a family tree, if a tree, is a conifer

so that autumn could be all the time, or never

the tree won't tell, in its boast of narrow leaves,

ever green

Nc6

if my father is branch

if I, needle

if (and not if) we buried the runt-pup near the cattails

if (and not if) it was his suggestion, or my

cone-pride—needle & branch

3. Bc4

green   behind the ear; thumb; with envy (with *vie!*)
         the year behind you (as an owner with his pet and a leash)
         the year that lashes
         that possesses you as photosynthesis a leaf

        chlorophyll   a plant-calorie
   what makes blonde hair green   is chlorine

        quiche "Florentine" involves spinach, wilted
        (and this is good—to wish the wilt)

whist   . . . in which two pairs of people try to take the majority of cards
tryst   . . . in which a pair tries to make a majority between them—
        to stomach the world (*monde*) between them

mondegreens   a (albeit) happy mishearing, which leads to an alternate universe of
        understanding (father : father) father-fodder)

Bc5

Why not inherit precision, like an eye color
or jaw-line?

That magnifying glass, an extra stub

among his fingers—

a carbon speck suspended in a diamond.

I know that(s):

Rolex, its second hand a giveaway, a handout hand—
time seeps through, so very water.

In a fake, minutes domino and lay the hour flat.

Imitation: a desire to get away with it.

Why not inherit his indecision—to leave
a hole in my fence, and a murmur.

4. b4

Small methods of control—

    pack a week before trips

    measure out a cup of cereal each morning

    count to one-hundred-and-twenty at the end of each shower

    (one to one-hundred-and-ten, hot water; the last ten seconds, cold)

to train oneself—

    food is a necessity rather than delight

    touch is most enjoyable from one's own hand

to learn the game is not about not—

losing. One's often trained by playing

simultaneously white and black sides:

hand *and* quiver, mouth *and* taste.

Bxb4

If a window's rolled down it's not tempting to fling open the door.

5. c3

Cities are crosswords we cram into:

In an alley, some one balanced me
against a brick wall.
A bra hook clawed into my spine.
I pressed close as a scar to the wall
where a saddle-shaped hook rode a scar
into my spine.

To match a definition of home,
but with a body too long—

one: single, individual,
odd, uncommon.

all one: making no difference,
insignificant.

won: to have carried out defeat

won: to have become number one,

world champion.

(a title splits the individual from the everyman)

6. d4

Divided a self into worlds:

city, city, the heart,

the head. I used the same name

in all of them. The same mouth.

It wasn't easy, remembering who

of me wanted what, and who.

Each afraid I might forget her.

exd4

move: to stir the emotions, to transfer, to act, to settle.

move on: to leave, or change.

Father Of
Father Of Chess Of This Chest
Farther From This Chest is my love than I would want him
First, an hour away Then a sea
Four states over on the ribcage of this country we fondle now
counting four states over and back
Father Who Art Who Is Art
I confess to the meat fallen in my mouth
off the day-bone dangled there
Father Who Imposes Father Whom I Superimpose
on myself toward my love to further us further

d3

Argument for long distance relationships—*your body cannot dictate where your soul resides.*

Argument against—*nomads.*

8. Qb3

The liver was once thought to store
memory, thus the popular saying
we drink to forget.

Qf6

Memory: a collector's Smurf glass
shattering like bone
with bones

thrown down the stairs.
Memory: Twelve steps to free
Krispie Kreme donuts
Memory:
Remembering: to celebrate inaccuracy

9. e5

time is the hand god fondles us with

Qg6

A demon possessed my dream,
I woke to he who mumbled a Latin prayer—
softest nightlight of words.

10. Re1

There are days I would stand
in an offering plate—having nothing
else.

Nge7

every amateur and champion should have _____ memorized by heart

11. Ba3

The first time? No.

No, though I had
practiced. Having

caught bodies
moving together
like cursive letters
across a bed.

In awe, when my sister and I played
house, I asked to be
husband. We lined the shower with pillows,
moved up and down on one
another's thigh—little moans clinging to the tile.
A kind of knock-knock joke, this happiness.

b5

When one *knocks on wood*

that wood is most frequently

a table, whose parent is tree,

whose grains are weaved through it

like genes. When one *knocks*

on wood, a door is least frequently

that wood, for fear jinx

will be home, and answer it.

12. Qxb5

A child's prayer to the bathroom door
her mother hides behind:

O, divider. Praise your single tooth
sliding into its jaw.

Grow roots around she who crouches
there.

Sing praise to the mirror sky holds up to space.
May he who shoulders you get lost

in the noose of your grain.
Keep this room small.

Praise the knob that will not turn its cheek.
That preoccupies his hand.

Amen.

Rb4

he did get
he did   through

13. Qa4

after dinner
we counted cows

(cows blacked out the pastures)

a herd of grass

one made it through
the fence

(cows still filled us)

the herd divides like hair sections

I recounted two times
before I noticed

(cows fled us, they spread us to larger)

the grazing field is the body

Bd6

body a hyphen on the field
a hyphen fended off between us
as is the trend with compound words
compounded in this small intestine this line .

if we if now parenthesis
what addendum interrupted
what we might combine to
circle the culprit the thief of our circle

14. Nbd2

The palm reader scanned
my left hand, the one that signifies

health—*how much do you want*
to know?—Everything.—
Where do hands go? when?

                    Bb7

Amenorrhea: (the end
of a prayer, which means a petition
or the slightest chance) –er-re-uh.

Cervical dysplasia: display
(feet in stirrups) she- (pronoun
of female, or one who produces
ova and bears young) –uh.

Infertile, or unproductive—
antonym: prolific—producing
abundant results.

                    15. Ne4

We prank-call the doctor—

This truce.

                    Qf5

A skull half-buried in night—

the sun shovels warm bones across us.

The pup's unfinished scalp

moons through its dark fur—its brain

a bullet point—a bullet pointed

toward it. My love wasn't

disappointed by the moon.

But the sky, too large around it—

his robe around me, the sash double-wrapped.

What a lie—delicacy. A—delightful lie.

16. Bxd3

A man watched people
's reactions as they passed a dead pigeon
on the sidewalk he killed for the pleasure
of their discomfort—
his smile spread like a wing.
I put my hand on the bird,

Qh4

Interrogators say when a person is lying
he blinks more. Mangled tongue
harangued by eyes.

17. Nfb+

Does it count if the cone doesn't fall—
needle-hammocked, instead

gxf6

Or a cone's rolled in peanut butter, then birdseed,
and re-hung in a tree, where

hunger makes it a cone again.

18. exf6

a young game is one in which neither player has the advantage

a pathetic game is one in which a player loses in under twenty moves

a beautiful game depends on the principle
                              of truth which is the basis of all beauty
                              of harmony of proportion
                              of profundity of goal seeking
                              of rapturous satisfaction

Rg8

young, *e.g.*   I drew myself like a bath
pathetic, *e.g.*   so he wouldn't suspect
                             how little I wanted him—
beautiful, *e.g.*   this unkindness felt kind.

19. Rad1

My car joins the traffic-syringe—
each stop light, a skin to push through.
Another way in.

Qxf3

takes-the-edge-off versus forms-a-new-edge

20. Rxe7+

A suspension bridge
I couldn't cross
without queasiness—

Nxe7

my head between my knees, my heart—

21. Qxd7+

the voice on the answering machine
was gravelly, which accentuated
the ominous

the way the sound engineer engineers
a tire-tread-disheveling-gravel sound
to clue the viewer in
the car approaching is also encroaching

the voice again
every aisle stocked with the same *hello*

Kxd7

When the king is put in a series of checks without mate resulting, it's called
stalking.

22. Bf5+

Living together
is one move closer
to living apart.

Ke8

a *no vacancy* sign, and
what's turned away
is justified

a *no vacancy* sign
on the heart, though
it has four chambers,

which implies
a turnover
in affection

23. Bd7+

On a strand of DNA, 64 cellular hexagrams.

A ladder by which you enter the house built into the family tree.

Kd8

On the chessboard, 64 squares.

Of which never more than half are filled.

24. Bxe7+#

The board on which he taught me
to play was a gift from his mother.

It came, piled with assorted cheeses,
melting through their foil

(the scalp again) (the moon)
(his mouth opened up like a note

tacked to the door) (*I intended to come*)
(knock, knock) (a note tacked to the door

instead of an answer) (the *I* intentional)
what knife did he use that left no marks?

(*I* a blade slid from its you-case)
(what did you use, He?) (what has I left?)

Match

My slip's scrawled with the last time you undressed me. I've memorized
the distance you thumbed between

> —as if a thumb weren't always between us,
> to now wish me elastic, that I might snap back.

How could we be opponents before we opposed one another?
The moon, after all, is only a moon.

> You called it a quarter pulled from behind

—night pooled into what I thought was you, but was only lack of resistance
from the ceiling.

> Lack lacks you, subtitles programmed across the bottom of
> an illiterate sleep.

To say the sea backhands a rock sets up a pecking order—

> isn't your verb what denies
> the rock a strong beak—a rock hands back the sea.

Do you notice first the delicate handle, or loose bristles
of foam rebunched along the wave?

> The landscape was a brush cleaned out. We were
> on a beach waiting for a train.
> Someone peddled cokes.

You coaxed the petals to fold back to *is*.
We shared one.

> We were a unit before untied.

55

Love made you a small room I didn't want.

                     I didn't want to make love to you in the small room.
           There was a dead spider on the windowsill when I came back
              from shopping. I surprised you with flowers you fed
                       the spider into.

Glutton!—what you call *feed!*—even a mouth makeshifts a tomb.

              What sympathy did you loan when my own cells rebelled?

The cold washcloth I held to your head.

                  A body divides and conceives a miracle.

You confuse revision with division.

                  Bring in the magician, bring in the saw.

To un-calendar the day of me!

                       How else stay a body
        loose with desire you too preciously balance on a tray, so
                even little splashes, disaster.

A glass of milk reminds me of you in winter
spilled over our sheets.

                You were milk dressed up as snow.
      I put on the dress you left, then dropped marinara in my lap
              into flower shapes you'd like.

Forgetting must be the opposite of sun.

And *mine* the opposite of *mine*.

A waiter tied that red balloon to your chair, and we were

—I asked someone to picture us, to take
a picture, and you stopped smiling. So like a battery.

Nevermind was a tourist in our dialogue—you could
have guided it.

in Order of Alphabet Rather than Worth

(piece)

Tongue flops in the cartoon-dead
diagonal as a mountainside one might climb
to proclaim

the thing that revs like an engine in your
heart (conviction a confection peddled by . . .). Words are not alone
in their usefulness—

I remember distinctly your eye's effect: the pupil
and its crosshair shift. Vision invades—

this many blinks bankroll a lie. In the confessional
deposit your tongue.

Look is an eye's disciple, look:

windows differentiate the view from
the landscape; such particular gloss on your eyes today.

A shadow tattles the shape its object dictates:
prick or stab dependent on distance
not thrust—

skin must seem a bother
to knives: shrubs hiding a house, a hassle to push aside, but not
a problem. How quaint of the heart to keep so much blood
at home.

You have a rites right:

one bishop is the king's consultant, and one, the queen's.
One does not consult one—conspiracy bypassed
by color restriction: to say to the flake

you may fall anywhere
but in the snow.

(piece)

It must be a very old king,

that one step is the maximum

he can muster. Shadow his only touch form,

his transparent finger that falls

into his pawn fence,

his defensive position.

A mountain lion's tooth, that sensation station!—

three thousand more nerves

than bud the human hand.

What I mean is: if your skin already

constitutes my necessity.

A fetishist hired a crew of ten

to lion-wire his mouth—

pleasure a denture set

glassed beside the bed.

Success would have meant

the neck pulse dog-whistled

and the blood-rabbit

chased through its track.

The king is the board's largest artery.

Castle and the clot dissipates.

The plot's shovel

retracted—the dirt in your hand

won't be necessary:

the bull's-eye has a *die* requirement.

This, of course, presents the king as prevented

from offense

though he can attack any piece,

save the enemy king:

save in its exceptional case,

its anything-but.

Memory is the brain-sky—

how many constellations

can you point to?

I request a galaxy raise.

When a star is the precedent,

reach is invigorated with maybe-ness—

Orion's elbow can't exceed

a forearm from his wrist.

(piece)

The only piece with spring—its own season of capture.
    Jester—the hidden-room-behind-the-bookshelf movement:
        here's the floor plan, but—. A trophy kill hung upon the enemy wall:

eye-move spook, tagged no matter where you pace—
    a taxidermist's demise: he stuffs the stuff "haunt" forms from:
        guts spirit his hands, smear his canvas apron. The conundrum is worth:

bishop or knight? It's a quiet matter: a finger barbed
    against your plateaued lips or your hand a muzzle
        for the offender: who aces the close range game? The way dark

compacts vision to inches—then the streetlight invention.
    The personal sun of a bulb. When I draw you in squares
        you are too many to be accurate. The knight motion-traces its shape:

two squares for its neck, one square for its head.
    Are you mastered by your movement—*I'm well*
        a hip jut, and a pulse equivalent heel-toed in your step.

Envy its stubborn: obstruction struck dumb—
    clothes do so little to spoil our in-the-know of under clothes.
        Self ordered a guilt restraint, longing ankled in concrete:

there's a way out not squirm related.
    Ventriloquists provide a fine illustration:
        mouth gated for show rather than function.

(piece)

If you're for me, pawn the line: you can save
one point if sentimental, my hold-tight.

If you're for me, a closed-mouth yawn:
your fold-out bed, folded-in face.

If you're against me,
why can't I feel you.

The swoosh signifies a sword: a diagonal slice
outs more innards: curtains are easy to close.

If you're for me, the pawns branch, and the branches
don't olive. Enter these camps choice sleeps in:

don't mis-see branch
for wing: a dove doesn't belong;

mis-see branch for wing: caw is more menacing
than coo and without the peace connotation.

If against *me,* a letter count can't solve this:
you, tag-teamed, and *then*—

(piece)

The starting square is a cloak that completes its carve: monochrome.

Monosexed: pre-equality, the queen minus her queen particular parts: Prime Minister.

Then change administered: Thank you, Catherine, and you too, Elizabeth.

Mother, the board is yours.

The becoming piece: a pawn's metamorphosis.

Reminiscence is accidental: Henry the Eighth's wife-fest.

Polygamy occurs, but infrequently—

the difference between pants and a skirt is each leg acknowledged, or not.

Walking is such a diplomatic activity,

that feet so naturally hand back and forth their charge.

(piece)

Wormholes in each corner: that's the rapidity
of their transport—unwalled, the enemy should be uneasy.
Sixty fattens by four, and the chessboard's the *n*th-dimension.
I intuit there's something to it—*pawn* is a tongue's quick fix of *minutemen:*
a possessive procures fewer syllables than your name, so I'll call you
my before our grain-garbed seconds are drained. In an end game,
two rooks uproot a queen's supremacy—glove-block,

and the other glove clocks: there's time again—*again*
a tautology given the circular property time's faced with—
what I mean is, short hair and a round jaw line: *no* an aesthetic,
no as in let the minutes bang. Castling: the rook ears and the king tucks behind.
Castle: the rook's name exchanged for its shape—to call your body a body:
the objectification complaint; the compliment's admiration.
Air has airs about its claim to you: see goose bumps
it incites in your arena, see the wave.

Immortal Game

We hymn our way past the guard, and you,
there again, in your loosest shirt
reserved for wash day.

I've made a chair for you like
you like, its legs grafted from orange trees.
This is not our first yard,

that yard obscured beneath bulldozers.
In the same way your skin
as it dozes your field—your eye and eye and

why pores can't decide
if bonfire or
smother defines them.

Again: a booth between us, like an atom partition
elements endure. We split, and what happens is not
extraordinary—

the scientist disinterested,

we go un-
recorded.

History is imported through an I.
I cargo you here:

a glacier counseled your face in modesty—
hair combed, and the bulk
of your face beneath it.

Over our panes, aluminum foil you tacked.
Light slow to show through. Light unlike a vein.

Even night questioned itself.

What morning did you not kiss my eyelids
to wake me and whisper *tomb tomb*.

A vacant eye elicits praise—you pressed your fingers
into my sockets so I couldn't blink:

my mirror broken without skin to replenish its glaze.

I could not find your face. By extension, neither could I
your body. That strange absence—my Alcatraz eye
you bellied out of.

Don't think you did not teach me: I know now
you were cast well, fantastic stone.

A mannequin I spent Saturdays at estate sales to find,
dismantled, by you, insistent on hangers, wires bent
to a dialect of Latin—so clothes depend
on the body to shape them.

Yeast that arouses the dough.

I scalpel a frog I've named History—
instead of a paperclip, I remove from its belly

is. The past tense isn't welcome, or already travels
like an enzyme into our currency, this current body.

A pigeon ducks through the window
What didn't mold of the pita
in a bag nearby.

You manna it through the door.
I knock with each finger—my hand
five hands.

if you call me manna I will break myself open

pain (English), acutely unpleasant physical discomfort, or
(French), bread

I will break myself open and feed you

We dine this way—with blistered hands.

We climb through the imitation cave.
We hold ourselves like whole notes
in the mouth of the cave.

A choir acquires voices, and
white robes—your gums
the rack from which they hang.
From there, dress me—
my nude throat, stripped
its undergarment of song.

My coveted keyboard, a convent I go to with my fingers, my little clan.

A sermon there—committed to memory, permitted a mega-

byte to gnaw into permanence:

> Parentheses are hands in the whisper-act.
>
> A prayer list excuses parentheses from hands.
>
> The Alpha extends to the Alphabet and
>
> is guaranteed disciples by words' letter-dependency.
>
> How hyphens nail a-l-t-a-r together.
>
> How nails dash through a palm like a monosyllable.
>
> Italics word the voice off the page:
>
> Where was it we slept to—I want to say Barcelona.
>
> *Barcelona.*
>
> Within context, be wary the con. Tab, and shift.
>
> A back slash and front slash flap into prayer.

which of us insists Mozart's *Requiem in D Minor*
a God-sloshed prayer
you tilt your head to hear
to shape your ear into a sink

we bet on His etiquette
the spitting out

Why not glass rings—
that hand would ration hold more rationally.

I collect the shatter.
The implication: my motivation to cause it.

A certain amount of crying justifies sad:
I have this jar chiseled to full, and this face—

The postcarded psalm,
now a wing useless on a stair
without an ear to muscle it—

& bone peeking through like wind

as when

In this version of heaven,
there are versions of heaven.

In this, sixty-four—heavens?
Or is sixty-four the good number:
how many are heavening, as if picnicking.

In this heaven, you stuff leaves
in my pants because I cannot leave
for the house—I red the leaves.

Next: the left margin is prodigal,
a margin that's left.

In this version, snow mourns
tombstones, or tombstones
are warm enough to gland the effect.

Here, it is not the mailman
who delivers you.
No parceling back.

Do you take champagne on a picnic?
The cork released like a dove.
Or air a soft belly, gut-punched by doves.

In this, I
to the door
in the night-
gown you gowned
for me with chicken-wire
now weary in your closet.

This version of heaven's for heaven's sake.

Here, close your eyes
and put this in your mouth:
texture, or text-sure: feel
for your name
written, or not.
I've left directions in the rind.

This—god thinks he's funny.

Do you hear your hands?
A version of your hands?

This version of your hands
has octopus-dexterity;

this one, your wrecking-ball
thumbs, and whose ribs shine through their backs
like stained glass to aim for?

There is no calculator in your hands—

a grip in which I grid myself is this version: my precious point!

        In this version of heaven, fingers detach
                and course away.

      How many nests could be made with your hair alone?
      Chicken-wire me a nest, and I'll alone.

In this version, continents are foreheads
god oils across.

             Move your mouth to the other side than
             the chipped rim: in this version of
             heaven you don't throw out
             the glass.

The bones of God's hands are laid over the town.
One hundred and eight—an equivalent of bones in four human hands.
He throws them like pick-up sticks.
He bones the town.

      We move like calcium, absorbed, then disengaged with His bones.
      Sunday, and your bed—our bodies built up: a deposit.

He is more Divine Middle Ear: anvil, stirrup, and hammer.

      Which is father, and which son—

      the Ghost is easy: I balance my weight in *was*.

A billboard worth the passing,
we choose a longer route: *[h]appiness is submission to [g]od.*

Alice was last week's vandalism: *Happiness is Alice,* though my favorite: *Happiness is*
or is it *Happiness Was:*

loss is a matter of what will be missed: it's always repainted by
morning.

[props: a phone card & Saran wrap backlit by a lamp for sea-consistency,
placed between two speakers]

—Did you go to any museums?

—Churches.

—Mu-zee-uhms.
[repeating yourself slowly in case the connection were bad]

—Churches.

A coin transforms to light and validates
our indecision—you point to the clock,
mischievous halo secured around time.
A minute dissolves the light, like a wafer
lean on your tongue. Another coin's slipped in:
St. Catherine's head spins like a pig
on a spit we cease to salivate for. I carve a settlement
in this new emptiness, I move
my mouth in.

You shape your repentance
into a chessboard. A congregation of boards seep
around the pastor's feet like an inversion of rain.

Revoked for their intentions:
that the King be dethroned.

God is less rigorous
with his everywhere existence
in the dictionary—though a few words
are vessels: vernacular slings *king* from fair game.

Monopoly gets around its flaw, its endorsement
of material riches, with special editions:

three mangers trade inn.

It's a matter of adjustment: *my god* piloted to *my goodness,*
or *loose* to *your thighs open like a change-purse;*

thigh will be done.

We thumb the board open like a bible.
Under the table, my feet in your lap.
Your hand on my feet in your lap.

Every circumstance that may increase pleasure should be regarded;
and every action or word that is unfair, disrespectful, or that in any way may give uneasiness,
should be avoided.

Benjamin Franklin, *Morals of Chess*

Bad Etiquette:
Singing, Humming, & Other Forms of Music-Making

"the sensation of playing against Paul Morphy is as queer as the first electric shock, or chloroform"

Opera taught him how to operate
      a room like music

          to let instinct hover
above pieces like a planchette on a Ouija board.

A visceral whistle.

Hope disguises itself as prophesy: a surname
      predicts the sir it names—him, from

          chessplayer to lawyer to

      but no, a chessplayer is like a rose
in that it is itself and itself then more itself than his—
          self lost in the it of it.

      The one he wanted refused him.

      Her body unlike the board
          on which he so easily moved.

When touch is a throne with its seat torn out.

      A chess set commemorating
U.S. masters, sold first in 1954, with Morphy as king—"the first first-
          rate American player"—

his queen Liberty, her light bouquet, a torch heavy
      with light,
          a bouquet he never failed to buy

on Sunday walks. A gesture to
what can't be maintained.

Memory divides like rooks
        short-term and long—

        teamwork within a single mind.

Brain synapses dribble thought to the end
of the court

        to carry out the move.

                His trademark: center control,
        as with a dance-off,
rivals sidled.

                Soon, it's a craze—popularity defined by
                imitation.
        The Running Man the Robot

the Twist—

        when his mind slipped out of tune—
                        it was noise's weight,

        not a bow, the culprit of the snap.

Bad Etiquette:
To Indulge & Not Allow the Other Party
Those Indulgences

This must have been how it started,
Ms. H, the World's Most Compulsive Swallower,
her belly a flesh drawer,

forks, & knives,
several spoons,
947 pins—only 980 less than the year (1927 A.D.)
they were extracted.

If silverware is set before you, who's to blame
it's mistaken food.

Glass—at least it wasn't glass.
Metal a prerequisite for Mouth.

> *Ms. H, how did you break apart*
> *the spoons? Would it be too much to ask*
> *that I lay my head there—there upon your thimble?*

My mother every Christmas put sewing kits
in our stockings—I carried one in my pocket
without learning to sew.

That repair is possible
negates its necessity.

My fingers are nailed to the bite:
my love critiques the bad construction.

Ms. H, your preference is the precedent.
What's the gestation period of a blade?

It's a marvel—
swallow, and the throat's cocked.
Bullets & vitamins share their shape.

What false armor
skin is.

(nail: a claw) (nail clippings spit
around a digression)

I read about a man addicted to surgical removal—
first he traced his eyelids with a scalpel. The goal
to un-body himself—bone
the stud post
being hammers into.

Yes, I feel a little sorry

when we start a new game—all those pieces
poking out, & the board must ache
as if all that had been underneath it.

We re-set and trim its bones as we see fit to outfit our win.

Do you suppose that man kept the skin
once off him—
souvenirs.

Debris to build with.

I scatter myself across the floor—to whose
dismay, my habit inhabits this little room
my love wants space in.

Bad Etiquette:
Interruption

" . . . during the challenge in which Wilhelm Steinitz lost his title, his opponent complained of the noisiness with which he consumed his lemonade—in response, Steinitz asked for a refill."

Slurp. A lemon punctured
on the end of concentration—the last sip
in an ice corral. No thought sucked out.
Un-jam my brain gauge

jammed with not-knowing.
Suck it up, after mate—Steinitz led the applause,
his reign peeled off
like plastic over a photo i.d.—who are you
if not World Champion,

after 28 years. Loss a kind of divorce—
Mrs. reversed to *Miss,* unlike
I *miss* you. Unlike how he *missed*
the moves that would have kept a rook

from his king. I miss you.
Isn't it the elegant mouth
that would kiss its executioner's glove,

a slick spot near the thumb,
that those lips might later re-lip themselves
on a cheek to which they are held.

Notations, or
a day-count slashed into walls
like a rib diagram of a prostrate man.
Your body was a prayer mat
I pressed

myself into. Body that must be taken up
and carried, his crutches preceding legs:

pieces waiting for fingers to lead them.
Until delusions

shaped brainwaves into fingers—
his pieces no longer required touch to be
felt. What's touching—that it would
touch you? Imagine the ferry ride

to the asylum, light holding his face like a card
above the spilled stack
of waves, and under his arm, a pocket chess set—
host-skin, tick-cling. You left marks

on my neck as a brick path
leading away from a pool too cold to swim in.
Like all fools, he confessed
I imagine doctors are crazier than I. (Something-er than

I) At his logic's festival, rationale was booted
for toting a bootleg of sense
found in the pat-down. Where are you?

Play Resumed

Are you in chess?—Yes, I chess, I chess.

It is like this—the square a bed
where our pieces root in lieu of our bodies.

A torso sketch, such narrow shoulders.
Otherwise, a rectangle,

and my hand no need to go there

            —your teeth so very castellated.
So a safe decision: my tour of your mouth.

There are many hideouts along the ridge:
a cop car tucks itself in, a cop car shirts—

speed-yanked, your come-after-me need:
why out the corner of the eye can't satisfy

that the whole head heads toward the glimpse.

Notes

"the first chess-playing automaton: The Turk" owes gratitude to NPR for discussing Tom Standage's *The Turk*, a nonfiction book that was the jumping-off point and informant of this piece.

"The Correspondence Game" is also indebted to Standage and his ode to invention.

Fred Reinfeld's *The Human Side of Chess* was the primary source of information about the chess masters who appear in "Evergreen Game" and the "Bad Etiquette" poems.

Kristi Maxwell currently lives and writes in the birthplace of Kenneth Koch, though she calls Cleveland, Tennessee, and Tucson, Arizona, home. Her poems have appeared in *How2, LIT, the Modern Review, POOL, Spinning Jenny, Tarpaulin Sky, the tiny, Typo, Coconut,* and in various other publications.

Ahsahta Press

Sawtooth Poetry Prize Series

2002: Aaron McCollough, *Welkin* (Brenda Hillman, judge)

2003: Graham Foust, *Leave the Room to Itself* (Joe Wenderoth, judge)

2004: Noah Eli Gordon, *The Area of Sound Called the Subtone* (Claudia Rankine, judge)

2005: Karla Kelsey, *Knowledge, Forms, The Aviary* (Carolyn Forché, judge)

2006: Paige Ackerson-Kiely, *In No One's Land* (D. A. Powell, judge)

2007: Rusty Morrison, *the true keeps calm biding its story* (Peter Gizzi, judge)

New Series

1. Lance Phillips, *Corpus Socius*
2. Heather Sellers, *Drinking Girls and Their Dresses*
3. Lisa Fishman, *Dear, Read*
4. Peggy Hamilton, *Forbidden City*
5. Dan Beachy-Quick, *Spell*
6. Liz Waldner, *Saving the Appearances*
7. Charles O. Hartman, *Island*
8. Lance Phillips, *Cur aliquid vidi*
9. Sandra Miller, *Oriflamme*
10. Brigitte Byrd, *Fence Above the Sea*
11. Ethan Paquin, *The Violence*
12. Ed Allen, *67 Mixed Messages*
13. Brian Henry, *Quarantine*
14. Kate Greenstreet, *case sensitive*
15. Aaron McCollough, *Little Ease*
16. Susan Tichy, *Bone Pagoda*
17. Susan Briante, *Pioneers in the Study of Motion*
18. Lisa Fishman, *The Happiness Experiment*
19. Heidi Lynn Staples, *Dog Girl*
20. David Mutschlecner, *Sign*
21. Kristi Maxwell, *Realm Sixty-four*

Ahsahta Press

Modern and Contemporary Poetry of the American West

This book is set in Apollo MT type with Eurostile LT Standard titles
by Ahsahta Press at Boise State University
and manufactured according to the Green Press Initiative
by Thomson-Shore, Inc.
Cover design by Quemadura.
Book design by Janet Holmes.

AHSAHTA PRESS

2007

JANET HOLMES, DIRECTOR

STEFFEN BROWN

NAOMI TARLE

J R WALSH

DENNIS BARTON, INTERN

DALE SPANGLER, INTERN